Little Pebble™

Celebrate Spring
Flowers

by Kathryn Clay

raintree
a Capstone company — publishers for children

Raintree is an imprint of Capstone Global Library Limited, a company incorporated in England and Wales having its registered office at 264 Banbury Road, Oxford, OX2 7DY – Registered company number: 6695582

www.raintree.co.uk
myorders@raintree.co.uk

Edited by Erika L. Shores
Designed by Juliette Peters and Ashlee Suker
Picture research by Svetlana Zhurkin
Production by Katy LaVigne
Originated by Capstone Global Library
Printed and bound in China.

ISBN 978 1 4747 1237 8

19 18 17 16 15
10 9 8 7 6 5 4 3 2 1

British Library Cataloguing in Publication Data
A full catalogue record for this book is available from the British Library.

Acknowledgements
We would like to thank the following for permission to reproduce photographs: Dreamstime: Jean Schweitzer, 13; Shutterstock: Aksenya, 9, Andrew Mayovskyy, 7, Andrii Koval, 1, Catalin Petolea, 11, Creative Travel Projects, 17, Elena Shutova, 3, green space, 15, honzik7, 21, Nataliiap, cover, Peter Nanista, 19, Ryan Lewandowski, 5, USBFCO, back cover and throughout.

Every effort has been made to contact copyright holders of material reproduced in this book. Any omissions will be rectified in subsequent printings if notice is given to the publisher.

All the internet addresses (URLs) given in this book were valid at the time of going to press. However, due to the dynamic nature of the internet, some addresses may have changed, or sites may have changed or ceased to exist since publication. While the author and publisher regret any inconvenience this may cause readers, no responsibility for any such changes can be accepted by either the author or the publisher.

Contents

Spring is here!

Winter is over.

Spring is here.

We see colourful flowers.

Growing

Rain falls.

The Sun shines.

Plants need water
and sunlight.

Stems push up through soil.

Buds start to bloom.

All kinds of flowers

Purple petals open.

Jack looks at a crocus.

Look on the ground.

Ali finds a daisy.

Look in the tree.

Cherry blossoms grow.

Find a lilac bush.

Its flowers smell sweet.

Look in the garden.

Five tulips grow.

Ella smells red roses.

What flowers do
you see in spring?

Glossary

bloom   produce a flower

bud   part of a plant that turns into a leaf or flower

petal   one of the outer parts of a flower

stem   main body of a plant

Find out more

All About Flowers (All About Plants), Claire Throp
(Raintree, 2014)

Learning About Plants (The Natural World), Catherine Veitch
(Raintree, 2013)

Wild Flowers (The Great Nature Hunt), Cath Senker
(Franklin Watts, 2016)

Websites

www.education.com/worksheets/weather-seasons
Discover activities related to weather and seasons
on this website.

www.bbc.co.uk/education/clips/zv2qxnb
Watch a video to learn what plants need to grow.

www.sciencekids.co.nz/plants.html
Learn all about plants on this website.

Index